contents

NZ, Canada, US and UK readers
Please note that Australian cup and spoon
measurements are metric. A quick conversion
guide appears on page 63.

chicken chow mein

*Crispy fried noodles are sold packaged (commonly
a 100g packet), already deep-fried and ready to eat.
They are sometimes labelled crunchy noodles, and are
available in two widths – thin and spaghetti-like or wide
and flat like fettuccine. You will need a quarter of a large
chinese cabbage for this recipe.*

2 tablespoons peanut oil
600g chicken mince
2 cloves garlic, crushed
4cm piece fresh ginger (20g), grated
1 medium red capsicum (200g), sliced thinly
2 teaspoons cornflour
½ cup (125ml) chicken stock
¼ cup (60ml) soy sauce
5 green onions, sliced thickly
1 cup (80g) bean sprouts
2 cups (160g) finely shredded chinese cabbage
200g crispy fried noodles

Heat half of the oil in wok; stir-fry chicken,
in batches, until browned all over.
Heat remaining oil in same wok; stir-fry garlic,
ginger and capsicum until capsicum is just tender.
Blend cornflour with stock and sauce in small jug.
Return chicken to wok with cornflour mixture; stir-fry
until sauce boils and thickens. Add onion, sprouts
and cabbage; stir-fry until heated through. Serve
on crispy fried noodles.

serves 4
per serving 25.9g fat (7.2g saturated);
1795kJ (429 cal); 15.1g carb
tip Prawns can also be added to this recipe.
on the table in 30 minutes

sweet soy chicken with noodles

Kecap manis is an Indonesian sweet soy sauce which is available in most supermarkets and Asian food stores. We used hokkien noodles in this recipe, but any fresh wheat noodle, such as shanghai, can be substituted.

500g hokkien noodles
1 tablespoon peanut oil
750g chicken thigh fillets, sliced thickly
8 green onions, chopped coarsely
4 cloves garlic, crushed
2cm piece fresh ginger (10g), sliced thinly
230g can sliced water chestnuts, drained
300g choy sum, trimmed, chopped coarsely
2 tablespoons coarsely chopped fresh coriander
2 tablespoons kecap manis
¼ cup (60ml) chicken stock

Place noodles in medium heatproof bowl, cover with boiling water, separate with fork; drain.
Heat oil in wok; stir-fry chicken, in batches, until browned all over. Return chicken to wok with onion, garlic, ginger and water chestnuts; stir-fry until fragrant.
Add choy sum, coriander, kecap manis and stock; stir-fry until chicken is cooked through and choy sum just wilted. Serve noodles topped with chicken mixture.

serves 4
per serving 20g fat (5.3g saturated); 2761kJ (659 cal); 70.1g carb
serving suggestion For chilli lovers, serve this dish with sambal oelek.
on the table in 30 minutes

chicken and oyster sauce stir-fry

1 tablespoon sesame oil
1 tablespoon peanut oil
750g chicken thigh fillets, sliced thickly
175g broccolini, chopped coarsely
230g fresh baby corn, halved lengthways
2 cloves garlic, crushed
½ cup (125ml) oyster sauce
1 tablespoon rice wine vinegar
2 tablespoons water
½ cup coarsely chopped fresh garlic chives

Heat half of the combined oils in wok; stir-fry chicken, in batches, until cooked through.
Heat remaining oil in same wok, stir-fry broccolini, corn and garlic until vegetables are just tender.
Return chicken to wok with combined oyster sauce, vinegar and water until heated through. Stir in chives.

serves 4
per serving 21.1g fat (4.8g saturated);
1638kJ (391 cal); 17.1g carb
on the table in 25 minutes

spicy noodle, vegetable and chicken stir-fry

200g packet dried egg noodles
2 tablespoons vegetable oil
600g chicken breast fillets, sliced
1 large carrot (180g), sliced thinly
250g button mushrooms, sliced thickly
2cm piece fresh ginger (10g), grated
¼ cup (60ml) chicken stock
¼ cup (60ml) oyster sauce
2 tablespoons soy sauce
4 green onions, sliced thinly
2 long red chillies, sliced thinly
150g sugar snap peas

Cook noodles in large saucepan of boiling water. Drain; rinse under cold water.
Heat half of the oil in wok; stir-fry chicken, in batches, until just cooked through.
Heat remaining oil in same wok; stir-fry carrot, mushroom and ginger until vegetables are just tender.
Return chicken to wok with combined stock and sauces; stir-fry until hot. Add noodles, onion, chilli and peas; stir-fry until heated through.

serves 4
per serving 9.3g fat (1.5g saturated); 1373kJ (328 cal); 29.8g carb
on the table in 25 minutes

stir-fried chicken and gai larn

Gai larn, also known as gai lum or chinese broccoli, can be found in Asian food stores and many greengrocers.

2 tablespoons sesame oil
500g chicken thigh fillets, sliced thinly
2 teaspoons sambal oelek
190g can sliced water chestnuts, drained
227g can bamboo shoot strips, drained
1 large red capsicum (350g), sliced thinly
⅓ cup (80ml) kecap manis
500g gai larn, chopped coarsely
2 cups (160g) bean sprouts

Heat half of the oil in wok; stir-fry chicken, in batches, until cooked through.
Heat remaining oil in same wok; stir-fry sambal, water chestnuts, bamboo shoots and capsicum about 2 minutes or until capsicum is just tender.
Return chicken to wok with kecap manis and gai larn; stir-fry until gai larn is just wilted. Remove from heat; stir in sprouts.

serves 4
per serving 18.8g fat (4.1g saturated); 1363kJ (326 cal); 9g carb
on the table in 25 minutes

chicken, chilli and kaffir lime stir-fry

2 tablespoons vegetable oil
500g chicken breast fillets, sliced thinly
2 medium zucchini (240g), sliced thinly
4cm piece fresh ginger (20g), grated
6 green onions, sliced thickly
½ cup (125ml) water
2 tablespoons lime juice
¼ cup (60ml) oyster sauce
¼ cup (60ml) sweet chilli sauce
5 kaffir lime leaves, shredded
1 cup loosely packed fresh thai basil leaves
3 cups (240g) bean sprouts

Heat half of the oil in wok; stir-fry chicken,
in batches, until browned lightly.
Heat remaining oil in same wok; stir-fry zucchini,
ginger and onion until zucchini is just tender.
Return chicken to wok with combined water,
juice, sauces and lime leaves; stir-fry until chicken
is cooked through. Add basil and bean sprouts;
stir-fry until combined.

serves 4
per serving 13.4g fat (2g saturated);
1219kJ (291 cal); 9.9g carb
on the table in 25 minutes

curried chicken and coconut stir-fry

2 tablespoons peanut oil
700g chicken thigh fillets, sliced thinly
1 large brown onion (200g), sliced thinly
2 cloves garlic, crushed
¼ cup (60g) madras curry paste
3 medium egg tomatoes (225g), chopped coarsely
1 cup (250ml) coconut cream
½ cup (125ml) chicken stock
2 tablespoons coarsely chopped fresh coriander
1 teaspoon brown sugar
2 tablespoons lemon juice

Heat half of the oil in wok; stir-fry chicken,
in batches, until cooked through.
Heat remaining oil in same wok; stir-fry onion
and garlic until onion is just tender. Add curry
paste; stir-fry until fragrant.
Return chicken to wok with tomato, coconut
cream, stock, coriander, sugar and juice; stir-fry
until heated through.
Serve with naan bread, basmati rice or
pappadums, if desired.

serves 4
per serving 40.3g fat (17.5g saturated);
2269kJ (542 cal); 9.3g carb
on the table in 25 minutes

prawn and bok choy stir-fry

1.2kg large uncooked prawns
2 tablespoons sesame oil
1 clove garlic, crushed
1 large yellow capsicum (350g), sliced thickly
400g baby bok choy, quartered lengthways
¼ cup (60ml) water
¼ cup (60ml) kecap manis
2 tablespoons soy sauce
½ cup coarsely chopped fresh coriander

Shell and devein prawns, leaving tails intact.
Heat half of the oil in wok; stir-fry garlic and
capsicum until tender. Add prawns; stir-fry until
just changed in colour. Remove from wok.
Heat remaining oil in wok; stir-fry bok choy
until just wilted.
Return prawn mixture to wok with remaining
ingredients; stir-fry until prawns are cooked through.

serves 4
per serving 10.5g fat (1.5g saturated);
1160kJ (277 cal); 11.1g carb
on the table in 30 minutes

prawn, scallop and lime stir-fry

500g large uncooked prawns
1 tablespoon sesame oil
2 cloves garlic, crushed
2cm piece fresh ginger (10g), grated
1 fresh red thai chilli, sliced thinly
250g broccolini, chopped coarsely
200g asparagus, chopped coarsely
300g scallops
2 tablespoons lime juice
2 tablespoons soy sauce
4 green onions, sliced thinly

Shell and devein prawns, leaving tails intact.
Heat oil in wok; stir-fry garlic, ginger and chilli
until fragrant. Add broccolini and asparagus;
stir-fry until just tender.
Add prawns and scallops; stir-fry until just cooked
through. Add remaining ingredients; stir-fry until hot.

serves 4
per serving 6.9g fat (0.9g saturated);
1874kJ (448 cal); 62.7g carb
tip Substitute gai lam or broccoli if broccolini
is not available.
on the table in 30 minutes

pad thai

500g thick fresh rice noodles
12 medium uncooked prawns (540g)
1 tablespoon peanut oil
2 eggs, beaten lightly
1 tablespoon water
400g pork mince
1 large brown onion (200g), sliced
2 cloves garlic, crushed
½ cup (125ml) sweet chilli sauce
1 tablespoon soy sauce
2 tablespoons fish sauce
⅓ cup (50g) toasted peanuts
2 cups (160g) bean sprouts
¼ cup firmly packed fresh coriander leaves

Place noodles in large heatproof bowl, cover with boiling water, separate with fork; drain. Meanwhile, shell and devein prawns, leaving tails intact.
Heat 1 teaspoon of the oil in wok; pour in half of the combined egg and water. Swirl heated wok to make a thin omelette and cook until set. Transfer omelette to chopping board, roll up tightly and cut into thin strips. Repeat with 1 teaspoon oil and remaining egg mixture.
Heat half of the remaining oil in same wok; stir-fry pork, onion and garlic until pork is lightly browned. Remove from wok.
Heat remaining oil in wok; stir-fry prawns until almost cooked through. Add noodles, combined sauces, pork mixture and remaining ingredients; stir fry until prawns are cooked through.

serves 4
per serving 22.1g fat (5g saturated); 2811kJ (672 cal); 68.5g carb
on the table in 30 minutes

crisp beef with gai larn

2 tablespoons cornflour
½ teaspoon bicarbonate of soda
500g beef strips
½ cup (125ml) peanut oil
¼ cup (60ml) sweet chilli sauce
2 tablespoons soy sauce
1 clove garlic, crushed
1 teaspoon sesame oil
1 large red onion (300g), sliced thinly
½ small chinese cabbage (400g), shredded coarsely
400g gai larn, chopped coarsely

Combine cornflour and soda in large bowl. Add beef; toss to coat all over, shaking off excess.
Heat a third of the peanut oil in wok; stir-fry about a third of the beef until crisp. Drain on absorbent paper; cover to keep warm. Repeat with remaining peanut oil and beef.
Combine sauces and garlic in small bowl.
Heat sesame oil in same cleaned wok; stir-fry onion until just tender. Add cabbage and gai larn; stir-fry 1 minute. Add sauce mixture and beef; stir-fry until heated through.

serves 4
per serving 34.4g fat (7.6g saturated); 2182kJ (521 cal); 16.1g carb
on the table in 30 minutes

beef kway teow

So popular in Singapore and throughout the Malay peninsula that they're practically regarded as fast food, kway teow are fresh, flat, wide rice noodles fried with meat or seafood and assorted vegetables.

2 tablespoons peanut oil
500g beef strips
450g fresh wide rice noodles
3 cloves garlic, crushed
2cm piece fresh ginger (10g), grated
6 green onions, cut into 2cm pieces
1 small red capsicum (150g), sliced thinly
2 cups (160g) bean sprouts
¼ cup (75g) satay sauce
2 tablespoons fish sauce

Heat half of the oil in wok; stir-fry beef, in batches, until browned all over.
Place noodles in large heatproof bowl, cover with boiling water, separate with fork; drain.
Heat remaining oil in same wok; stir-fry garlic and ginger until fragrant. Add onion and capsicum; stir-fry until vegetables are just tender. Return beef to wok with noodles, sprouts and sauces; stir-fry until heated through.

serves 4
per serving 19.3g fat (5g saturated); 2231kJ (533 cal); 54.2g carb
on the table in 25 minutes

mee goreng

*Mee goreng simply translates as fried noodles, and is
an everyday dish in Indonesia and Malaysia.*

600g hokkien noodles
1 tablespoon peanut oil
3 eggs, beaten lightly
500g beef strips
2 cloves garlic, crushed
2cm piece fresh ginger (10g), grated
500g baby bok choy, chopped coarsely
4 green onions, sliced thinly
¼ cup coarsely chopped fresh coriander
2 tablespoons dried shrimp
¼ cup (60ml) kecap manis
2 teaspoons sambal oelek
¼ cup (60ml) beef stock
½ cup (75g) toasted unsalted peanuts

Place noodles in large heatproof bowl, cover with
boiling water, separate with fork; drain.
Heat a quarter of the oil in wok; cook half of the egg,
tilting pan, until egg mixture is almost set. Remove
omelette from wok; repeat with another quarter of the
oil and remaining egg. Roll omelettes; slice thinly.
Heat remaining oil in same wok; stir-fry beef, garlic
and ginger, in batches, until beef is browned all over.
Place bok choy in same wok; stir-fry until just wilted.
Return beef mixture to wok with noodles, onion,
coriander, shrimp and combined kecap manis,
sambal and stock; stir-fry until heated through.
Serve topped with omelette and peanuts.

serves 4
per serving 24.1g fat (5.4g saturated);
3350kJ (800 cal); 91.8g carb
on the table in 25 minutes

beef and black bean stir-fry

2 tablespoons peanut oil
700g beef strips
200g green beans, cut into 5cm lengths
1 medium carrot (120g), sliced thinly
1 medium red capsicum (200g), sliced thinly
1 clove garlic, crushed
¼ cup (60ml) beef stock
¼ cup (60ml) black bean sauce
4 green onions, sliced thinly
230g can bamboo shoots, drained

Heat half of the oil in wok; stir fry beef, in batches, until browned all over.
Heat remaining oil in same wok; stir fry beans, carrot, capsicum and garlic until vegetables are just tender.
Return beef to wok with remaining ingredients; stir-fry until hot.

serves 4
per serving 21.6g fat (7g saturated); 1664kJ (398 cal); 8.5g carb
on the table in 20 minutes

beef

pepper beef and mushroom stir-fry

700g beef strips
2 teaspoons cracked black pepper
2 teaspoons ground sichuan pepper
2 tablespoons vegetable oil
1 medium brown onion (150g), sliced thickly
2 cloves garlic, crushed
100g shiitake mushrooms, halved
100g oyster mushrooms, halved
200g button mushrooms, halved
2 teaspoons cornflour
1 tablespoon water
⅓ cup (80ml) mirin
¼ cup (60ml) soy sauce

Combine beef and peppers in medium bowl;
toss to coat beef in pepper mixture.
Heat half of the oil in wok; stir-fry beef, in batches,
until browned all over.
Heat remaining oil in same wok; stir-fry onion and
garlic until onion is just tender. Add mushrooms;
stir-fry until mushrooms are just tender.
Add blended cornflour and water, then mirin and
sauce; stir-fry until mixture boils and thickens slightly.
Return beef to wok; stir-fry until heated through.

serves 4
per serving 20.3g fat (5.2g saturated);
1571kJ (375 cal); 5.3g carb
tip Dry sherry may be used instead of mirin.
on the table in 30 minutes

spinach and beef stir-fry

2 tablespoons peanut oil
700g beef strips
2 cloves garlic, crushed
250g broccolini, chopped coarsely
300g enoki mushrooms
250g baby spinach leaves
¼ cup (60ml) beef stock
¼ cup (60ml) oyster sauce

Heat half of the oil in wok; stir-fry beef,
in batches, until browned all over.
Heat remaining oil in same wok; stir-fry garlic
and broccolini until just tender.
Return beef to wok with remaining ingredients;
stir-fry until spinach is just wilted.

serves 4
per serving 18.2g fat (5.3g saturated);
1514kJ (362 cal); 5.4g carb
on the table in 20 minutes

chilli pork with oyster sauce

1 tablespoon peanut oil
500g pork fillets, sliced thinly
1 clove garlic, crushed
1 medium white onion (150g), sliced thinly
1 large red capsicum (350g), sliced thinly
1 small green zucchini (90g), sliced thinly
1 small yellow zucchini (90g), sliced thinly
¼ cup (60ml) oyster sauce
1 tablespoon mild sweet chilli sauce
1 tablespoon coarsely chopped fresh
    coriander leaves

Heat oil in wok; stir-fry pork, in batches,
until browned all over.
Stir-fry garlic and onion until onion is just tender.
Add capsicum and zucchini; stir-fry until tender.
Return pork to wok with combined sauces;
stir-fry until hot. Serve sprinkled with coriander.

serves 4
per serving 8g fat (1.9g saturated);
986kJ (235 cal); 10.2g carb
on the table in 30 minutes

japanese pork stir-fry

2 tablespoons peanut oil
600g pork fillets, sliced thinly
1 large brown onion (200g), sliced thinly
1 medium red capsicum (200g), sliced thinly
1 medium green capsicum (200g), sliced thinly
200g green beans, chopped coarsely
2 cups (140g) coarsely shredded chinese cabbage
¼ cup (60ml) tonkatsu sauce
¼ cup (60ml) sukiyaki sauce

Heat half of the oil in wok; stir-fry pork, in batches, until browned all over.
Heat remaining oil in same wok; stir-fry onion until just tender. Add capsicums and beans; stir-fry until just tender.
Return pork to wok with cabbage and sauces; stir-fry until cabbage just wilts.

serves 4
per serving 12.8g fat (2.9g saturated); 1251kJ (299 cal); 7.5g carb
on the table in 25 minutes

thai-style pork and chilli noodles

1 tablespoon vegetable oil
600g pork fillet, sliced thinly
2 cloves garlic, crushed
1 fresh long red chilli, chopped finely
2 tablespoons fish sauce
¼ cup (60ml) kecap manis
⅓ cup (80ml) lime juice
200g dried egg noodles
8 green onions, sliced thinly
3 cups (240g) bean sprouts
⅓ cup coarsely chopped fresh coriander
4 kaffir lime leaves, shredded

Heat oil in wok; stir-fry pork until browned all over.
Add garlic and chilli; stir-fry until fragrant.
Add fish sauce, kecap manis and juice; stir-fry
until mixture boils and thickens slightly.
Meanwhile, cook noodles in large saucepan
of boiling water until tender; drain.
Add onion, bean sprouts and coriander to
pork mixture; stir until heated through. Toss
the pork mixture through the noodles; sprinkle
with lime leaves.

serves 4
per serving 14.4g fat (4g saturated);
1807kJ (432 cal); 38.5g carb
on the table in 30 minutes

sticky pork and vegetable stir-fry

¼ cup (60ml) peanut oil
600g pork fillets, sliced thinly
1 medium brown onion (150g), sliced thinly
2 cloves garlic, crushed
300g broccoli, chopped coarsely
230g baby corn, halved lengthways
2 medium carrots (240g), sliced thinly
⅓ cup (80ml) sweet chilli sauce
1 tablespoon brown sugar
2 tablespoons soy sauce

Heat half of the oil in wok; stir-fry pork, in batches, until browned all over.

Heat remaining oil in same wok; stir-fry onion and garlic until tender. Add broccoli, corn and carrot; stir-fry until just tender.

Return pork to wok with remaining ingredients; stir-fry until the mixture boils and thickens slightly.

serves 4
per serving 18.6g fat (3.9g saturated);
1738kJ (415 cal); 22.3g carb
on the table in 25 minutes

pork and singapore noodle stir-fry

250g dried thin egg noodles
2 tablespoons peanut oil
4 eggs, beaten lightly
1 tablespoon water
1 medium brown onion (150g), chopped finely
2 cloves garlic, crushed
2 tablespoons mild curry paste
200g pork mince
200g Chinese barbecued pork, sliced
200g shelled cooked small prawns
3 green onions, chopped coarsely
¼ cup (60ml) soy sauce
2 tablespoons oyster sauce
1 fresh long red chilli, chopped finely

Cook noodles in large saucepan of boiling water until just tender; drain.

Meanwhile, heat 2 teaspoons of the oil in wok; add half of the combined egg and water, swirl to make thin omelette. When egg is just set, remove omelette from wok, roll up and cut into thin strips. Repeat with 2 teaspoons of the oil and remaining egg mixture.

Heat remaining oil in same wok; stir-fry onion and garlic until onion is just tender. Add curry paste; stir-fry until fragrant.

Add pork; stir-fry until browned all over. Add half of the omelette strips and remaining ingredients; stir-fry until heated through. Serve topped with remaining omelette strips.

serves 4
per serving 30.5g fat (8.3g saturated);
2769kJ (662 cal); 52.3g carb
on the table in 30 minutes

lemon grass lamb in lettuce cups

8 iceberg lettuce leaves
100g rice vermicelli
2 tablespoons peanut oil
750g lamb strips
1 medium carrot (120g), sliced thinly
3 cloves garlic, crushed
4cm piece fresh ginger (20g), chopped finely
2 tablespoons finely chopped fresh lemon grass
4 fresh kaffir lime leaves, sliced thinly
1 tablespoon lime juice
¼ cup (60ml) sweet chilli sauce
¼ cup (60ml) fish sauce
¼ cup coarsely chopped fresh chives

Place lettuce in large bowl of iced water; stand
10 minutes. Drain; pat dry with absorbent paper.
Meanwhile, place vermicelli in large heatproof bowl;
cover with boiling water. Stand until just tender; drain.
Heat half of the oil in wok; stir-fry lamb, in batches,
until browned all over.
Heat remaining oil in same wok; stir-fry carrot,
garlic, ginger, lemon grass and lime leaves until
carrot is tender. Return lamb to wok with vermicelli,
juice, sauces and half of the chives; stir-fry until
heated through.
Place two lettuce leaves on each serving plate;
divide lamb mixture among leaves, sprinkle with
remaining chives.

serves 4
per serving 16.6g fat (4.7g saturated);
1548kJ (370 cal); 11.1g carb
on the table in 30 minutes

thai lamb and noodle stir-fry

200g thick rice stick noodles
2 tablespoons peanut oil
500g lamb strips
1 tablespoon finely chopped lemon grass
1 fresh long red chilli, sliced thinly
2 cloves garlic, crushed
1 large brown onion (220g), sliced thinly
250g snake beans, cut into 5cm lengths
1/3 cup (80ml) sweet chilli sauce
2 tablespoons fish sauce
1/4 cup (60ml) chicken stock
1/4 cup firmly packed fresh mint leaves
1/4 cup (35g) toasted salted peanuts

Place noodles in large heatproof bowl, cover with boiling water, stand until just tender; drain.
Meanwhile, heat half of the oil in wok; stir-fry lamb, in batches, until browned all over.
Heat remaining oil in wok; stir-fry lemon grass, chilli, garlic and onion until tender. Add beans; stir-fry until almost tender.
Return lamb to wok with sauces, stock and noodles; stir fry until hot. Add mint, toss gently. Serve immediately, sprinkled with peanuts.

serves 4
per serving 19.9g fat (4.3g saturated); 1774kJ (424 cal); 20.7g carb
on the table in 30 minutes

stir-fried lamb in hoisin sauce

2 tablespoons peanut oil
600g lamb strips
2 cloves garlic, crushed
2cm piece fresh ginger (10g), grated
1 medium brown onion (150g), sliced thinly
1 small red capsicum (150g), sliced thinly
1 small yellow capsicum (150g), sliced thinly
6 green onions, sliced thinly
⅓ cup (80ml) chicken stock
1 tablespoon soy sauce
¼ cup (60ml) hoisin sauce

Heat half of the oil in wok; stir-fry lamb,
in batches, until browned all over.
Heat remaining oil in same wok; stir-fry garlic,
ginger and brown onion until onion is just tender.
Add capsicums and green onion; stir-fry until
capsicum is just tender.
Return lamb to wok, add combined stock
and sauces; stir until sauce boils and thickens
slightly and lamb is cooked as desired.

serves 4
per serving 15.2g fat (4.2g saturated);
1316kJ (314 cal); 8.5g carb
on the table in 30 minutes

stir-fried greens with green beans

1 tablespoon sesame oil
2 cloves garlic, crushed
2cm piece fresh ginger (10g), grated
300g green beans, halved
8 green onions, chopped coarsely
500g spinach, chopped coarsely
600g baby bok choy, chopped coarsely
2 tablespoons soy sauce
1 tablespoon sweet chilli sauce
2 tablespoons finely chopped fresh coriander

Heat oil in wok or large frying pan; stir-fry garlic,
ginger, beans and onion until beans are just tender.
Add spinach and bok choy; stir-fry until bok choy
is just wilted. Add combined sauces; stir-fry until
hot. Serve sprinkled with coriander.

serves 4
per serving 5.5g fat (0.7g saturated);
433kJ (103 cal); 6.6g carb
on the table in 20 minutes

stir-fried vegetables and tofu in black bean sauce

500g firm tofu
2 tablespoons peanut oil
6 finger eggplant (360g), quartered lengthways
1 medium red capsicum (200g), sliced thinly
230g can sliced water chestnuts, rinsed, drained
2 cloves garlic, crushed
2cm piece fresh ginger (10g), grated
250g broccolini, chopped coarsely
500g choy sum, chopped coarsely
2 tablespoons kecap manis
⅓ cup (80ml) black bean sauce

Weight tofu between two boards; stand, tilted, 10 minutes. Cut tofu into 2cm cubes; pat dry between layers of absorbent paper.
Heat half of the oil in wok; stir-fry tofu, in batches, until lightly browned. Drain on absorbent paper; cover to keep warm.
Heat half of the remaining oil in same wok; stir-fry eggplant until soft. Add capsicum and water chestnuts; stir-fry until vegetables are just tender, remove from wok.
Heat remaining oil in wok; stir-fry garlic and ginger until fragrant. Add broccolini and choy sum; stir-fry until choy sum just wilts. Add combined sauces and eggplant mixture; stir-fry until heated through. Add tofu; toss gently to combine.

serves 4
per serving 13g fat (2.1g saturated); 919kJ (219 cal); 11.3g carb
on the table in 30 minutes

vegetable chap-chai

1 tablespoon peanut oil
1 clove garlic, crushed
4cm piece fresh ginger (20g), grated
150g tat soi, trimmed
200g choy sum, chopped coarsely
200g baby bok choy, chopped coarsely
200g chinese cabbage, chopped coarsely
150g sugar snap peas
2 tablespoons soy sauce
¼ cup (60ml) hoisin sauce

Heat oil in wok; stir-fry garlic and ginger
until fragrant.
Add tat soi, choy sum, bok choy, cabbage,
peas and combined sauces; stir-fry until
vegetables are just tender.

serves 4
per serving 6.4g fat (1g saturated);
536kJ (128 cal); 10.1g carb
on the table in 20 minutes

pumpkin, basil and chilli stir-fry

¼ cup (60ml) peanut oil
1 large brown onion (200g), sliced thinly
2 cloves garlic, sliced thinly
4 fresh small red thai chillies, sliced thinly
1kg pumpkin, chopped coarsely
250g sugar snap peas
1 tablespoon brown sugar
¼ cup (60ml) vegetable stock
2 tablespoons soy sauce
¾ cup loosely packed opal basil leaves
4 green onions, sliced thinly
½ cup (75g) roasted unsalted peanuts

Heat oil in wok; stir-fry brown onion, in batches, until browned and crisp. Drain on absorbent paper.
Stir-fry garlic and chilli in wok until fragrant. Add pumpkin; stir-fry until browned all over and just tender. Add peas, sugar, stock and sauce; stir-fry until sauce thickens slightly.
Remove from heat; toss basil, green onion and nuts through stir-fry until well combined. Serve topped with fried onion.

serves 4
per serving 28.2g fat (5g saturated);
1615kJ (386 cal); 21.3g carb
tip Opal basil can be replaced with regular basil.
on the table in 25 minutes

sweet chilli tofu stir-fry

300g firm tofu
2 tablespoons kecap manis
2 tablespoons peanut oil
500g hokkien noodles
2 cloves garlic, crushed
2 medium carrots (240g), sliced thinly
300g broccoli, chopped
6 green onions, chopped coarsely
½ cup (125ml) sweet chilli sauce
1 tablespoon lime juice
⅓ cup (50g) salted peanuts, chopped coarsely
2 tablespoons coarsely chopped fresh coriander

Cut tofu into 3cm cubes; place in medium bowl
with half of the kecap manis. Toss to coat tofu
in kecap manis.
Heat half of the oil in wok; stir-fry tofu gently,
in batches, until browned all over. Cover to
keep warm.
Rinse noodles under hot water to separate;
drain well.
Heat remaining oil in same cleaned wok; stir-fry
garlic and carrot until just tender. Add broccoli;
stir-fry until just tender.
Add green onion, noodles, sauce, remaining
kecap manis and juice; stir-fry until heated through.
Stir in tofu, peanuts and coriander.

serves 4
per serving 22.7g fat (3.5g saturated);
2640kJ (631 cal); 77.6g carb
on the table in 30 minutes

glossary

basil

   opal: has large purple leaves and a sweet, gingery flavour.

   thai: also known as horapa; has smaller leaves than sweet basil, as well as purplish stems and a slight aniseed taste.

bamboo shoots tender shoots of bamboo, available in cans; drain and rinse before use.

bean sprouts also known as bean shoots; assorted beans and seeds germinated for consumption. Readily available are: mung bean, soy bean, alfalfa and snow pea sprouts.

bicarbonate of soda also known as baking soda.

bok choy also known as bak choy, pak choi, chinese white cabbage or chinese chard; has a fresh, mild mustard taste. Use stems and leaves. Baby bok choy, also known as shanghai bok choy, is more tender than bok choy.

broccolini a cross between broccoli and chinese kale; sweeter than broccoli. Each stem is topped by a loose floret that resembles broccoli; from floret to stem, broccolini is completely edible.

capsicum also known as bell pepper or, simply, pepper. Discard membranes and seeds before use.

chilli, red thai small, medium-hot and bright red in colour.

chinese cabbage also known as peking or napa cabbage, wong bok or petsai. Elongated with pale, crinkly leaves.

choy sum also known as pakaukeo or flowering cabbage; has long stems, light leaves and yellow flowers and is eaten, stems and all.

coconut cream the first pressing from grated mature coconut flesh; available in cans and cartons.

coriander also known as pak chee, cilantro or chinese parsley; leafy, bright-green herb with a pungent flavour. The leaves, stems and roots of coriander can be used.

cornflour also known as cornstarch; used as a thickening agent in cooking.

curry pastes some recipes call for commercially prepared pastes of various strengths and flavours. Use whichever one you feel suits your spice-level tolerance best.

dried shrimp available from Asian grocery stores.

eggplant, finger small, elongated eggplant; also known as aubergine.

ginger also known as green or root ginger; the thick gnarled root of a tropical plant.

gai larn also known as gai larn, kanah, gai lum, chinese broccoli and chinese kale; appreciated more for its stems than its coarse leaves.

kaffir lime leaves also known as bai magrood; look like two glossy dark-green leaves joined end to end. Used fresh or dried in manner of bay or curry leaves. Dried leaves are less potent so double the quantity if you substitute them for fresh. A strip of fresh lime peel can be substituted for each kaffir lime leaf.

kecap manis a dark, thick, sweet soy sauce. Depending on brand, the sweetness is derived from the addition of either molasses or palm sugar.

lemon grass tall, clumping, lemon-smelling and -tasting, sharp-edged grass; use only the white lower part of stem.

mince also known as ground meat, as in chicken, pork, etc.

mirin a Japanese champagne-coloured cooking wine, made of glutinous rice and alcohol, used expressly for cooking; not to be confused with sake.

mushrooms

   button: small, cultivated white mushrooms with mild flavour.

   shiitake: when fresh are also known as chinese black, forest or golden oak mushrooms; although cultivated, have the earthiness and taste of wild mushrooms. When dried, they are known as donko or dried chinese mushrooms; rehydrate before use.

   enoki: long, thin, white mushrooms, with a delicate fruity flavour.

   oyster: also known as abalone; grey-ish mushroom shaped like a fan. Prized for their smooth texture and subtle, oyster-like flavour.

noodles

   crispy fried: crispy egg noodles packaged already deep-fried.

   dried egg: made from wheat flour and egg; range in size from very fine to wide.

   hokkien: also known as stir-fry noodles; fresh wheat noodles resembling thick, yellow-brown spaghetti needing no pre-cooking before use.

   rice stick: popular dried rice noodles available in different widths; all should be soaked in hot water until soft.

rice vermicelli: also known as sen mee, mei fun or bee hoon. Similar to bean thread noodles, only longer and made with rice flour instead of mung bean starch. Before using, soak dried noodles in hot water until soft, then boil them briefly (1-3 minutes) and rinse with hot water. You can also deep-fry the dried noodles until they're crunchy.

oil

peanut: pressed from ground peanuts; most commonly used oil in Asian cooking because of its high smoke point (capacity to handle high heat without burning).

sesame: made from roasted, crushed, white sesame seeds; a flavouring rather than a cooking medium.

vegetable: any of a number of oils sourced from plants rather than animal fats.

onion

green: also known as scallion or (incorrectly) shallot; an immature onion picked before the bulb has formed, having a long, bright-green edible stalk.

red: also known as spanish, red spanish or bermuda onion; a sweet-flavoured, large, purple-red onion.

prawn also known as shrimp.

pumpkin also known as squash.

sauces

black bean: Chinese sauce made from fermented soy beans and spices.

fish: also known as nam pla or nuoc nam; made from pulverised, salted, fermented fish; has a pungent smell and strong taste.

hoisin: a thick, sweet and spicy Chinese paste made from salted, fermented soy beans, onions and garlic; used as a marinade or baste, or to accent stir-fries and barbecued or roasted foods.

oyster: Asian in origin, this rich, brown sauce is made from oysters and their brine, cooked with salt and soy sauce, and thickened with starches.

soy: also known as sieu, is made from fermented soy beans.

sukiyaki: Japanese sauce made from soy sauce, sugar, sake and mirin; available from Asian grocery stores.

sweet chilli: comparatively mild, thin Thai sauce made from red chillies, sugar, garlic and vinegar.

teriyaki: a homemade or commercially bottled sauce usually made from soy sauce, mirin, sugar, ginger and other spices; it imparts a distinctive glaze when brushed on grilled meat.

tonkatsu: thick, fruity, spicy Japanese sauce; similar to any commercial barbecue sauce.

sambal oelek also ulek or olek. Indonesian in origin; a salty paste made from ground chillies and vinegar.

scallops bivalve molluscs with fluted shell and attached roe.

shrimp paste also known as trasi or blanchan; a strong-scented, very firm, preserved paste made of dried, salted shrimp. Must be chopped or sliced thinly, then wrapped in foil and roasted before use.

sichuan pepper also known as szechuan or chinese pepper; has distinctive peppery-lemon flavour and aroma.

snake beans long (about 40cm), thin, round, fresh green beans, Asian in origin, with a taste similar to green or French beans. Used most frequently in stir-fries, they are also called yard-long beans because of their length.

sugar, brown an extremely soft, fine granulated sugar retaining molasses for its characteristic colour and flavour.

sugar snap peas also known as honey snap peas; fresh small pea eaten whole, pod and all, similarly to snow peas.

tat soi also known as rosette, pak choy, tai gu choy and chinese flat cabbage; a variety of bok choy developed to grow close to the ground so it is easily protected from frost. Its dark green leaves are cut into sections rather than separated, and used in soups, braises and stir fries.

tofu also known as bean curd.

vinegar, rice wine made from fermented rice with no additives.

water chestnuts resemble a chestnut in appearance. They are small brown tubers with a crisp, white, nutty tasting flesh. Their crunchy texture is best experienced fresh, however canned chestnuts are more easily obtained and can be kept about a month, once opened.

zucchini also known as courgette.

index

conversion chart

MEASURES

One Australian metric measuring cup holds approximately 250ml, one Australian metric tablespoon holds 20ml, one Australian metric teaspoon holds 5ml.

The difference between one country's measuring cups and another's is within a two- or three-teaspoon variance, and will not affect your cooking results.

North America, New Zealand and the United Kingdom use a 15ml tablespoon.

All cup and spoon measurements are level. The most accurate way of measuring dry ingredients is to weigh them. When measuring liquids, use a clear glass or plastic jug with the metric markings.

We use large eggs with an average weight of 60g.

DRY MEASURES

METRIC	IMPERIAL
15g	½oz
30g	1oz
60g	2oz
90g	3oz
125g	4oz (¼lb)
155g	5oz
185g	6oz
220g	7oz
250g	8oz (½lb)
280g	9oz
315g	10oz
345g	11oz
375g	12oz (¾lb)
410g	13oz
440g	14oz
470g	15oz
500g	16oz (1lb)
750g	24oz (1½lb)
1kg	32oz (2lb)

LIQUID MEASURES

METRIC	IMPERIAL
30ml	1 fluid oz
60ml	2 fluid oz
100ml	3 fluid oz
125ml	4 fluid oz
150ml	5 fluid oz (¼ pint/1 gill)
190ml	6 fluid oz
250ml	8 fluid oz
300ml	10 fluid oz (½ pint)
500ml	16 fluid oz
600ml	20 fluid oz (1 pint)
1000ml (1 litre)	1¾ pints

LENGTH MEASURES

METRIC	IMPERIAL
3mm	⅛in
6mm	¼in
1cm	½in
2cm	¾in
2.5cm	1in
5cm	2in
6cm	2½in
8cm	3in
10cm	4in
13cm	5in
15cm	6in
18cm	7in
20cm	8in
23cm	9in
25cm	10in
28cm	11in
30cm	12in (1ft)

OVEN TEMPERATURES

These oven temperatures are only a guide for conventional ovens. For fan-forced ovens, check the manufacturer's manual.

	°C (CELSIUS)	°F (FAHRENHEIT)	GAS MARK
Very slow	120	250	½
Slow	150	275 – 300	1 – 2
Moderately slow	170	325	3
Moderate	180	350 – 375	4 – 5
Moderately hot	200	400	6
Hot	220	425 – 450	7 – 8
Very hot	240	475	9

Are you missing some of the world's favourite cookbooks

The Australian Women's Weekly cookbooks are available from bookshops, cookshops, supermarkets and other stores all over the world. You can also buy direct from the publisher, using the order form below.

MINI SERIES £2.50 190X138MM 64 PAGES

TITLE	QTY	TITLE	QTY	TITLE	QTY
4 Fast Ingredients		Curries		Pasta	
15-minute Feasts		Drinks		Pickles and Chutneys	
30-minute Meals		Fast Fish		Potatoes	
50 Fast Chicken Fillets		Fast Food for Friends		Risotto	
After-work Stir-fries		Fast Soup		Roast	
Barbecue		Finger Food		Salads	
Barbecue Chicken		From the Shelf		Seafood	
Barbecued Seafood		Gluten-free Cooking		Simple Slices	
Biscuits, Brownies & Biscotti		Ice-creams & Sorbets		Simply Seafood	
Bites		Indian Cooking		Skinny Food	
Bowl Food		Italian		Stir-fries	
Burgers, Rösti & Fritters		Jams & Jellies		Summer Salads	
Cafe Cakes		Kids Party Food		Tapas, Antipasto & Mezze	
Cafe Food		Last-minute Meals		Thai Cooking	
Casseroles		Lebanese Cooking		Thai Favourites	
Char-grills & Barbecues		Malaysian Favourites		Vegetarian	
Cheesecakes, Pavlovas & Trifles		Microwave		Vegetarian Stir-fries	
Chocolate		Mince		Vegie Main Meals	
Chocolate Cakes		Muffins		Wok	
Christmas Cakes & Puddings		Noodles		TOTAL COST	£
Cocktails		Party Food			

Photocopy and complete coupon below

Name _____

Address _____

_____ Postcode _____

Country _____ Phone (business hours) _____

Email*(optional) _____
*By including your email address, you consent to receipt of any email regarding this magazine, and other emails which inform you of ACP's other publications, products, services and events, and to promote third party goods and services you may be interested in.

I enclose my cheque/money order for £ _____

or please charge £ _____ to my:

☐ Bankcard ☐ Mastercard ☐ Visa ☐ American Express ☐ Diners Club

Card number | | | | | | | | | | | | | | | | | | |

Cardholder's signature _____ Expiry date ____ /____

To order: Mail or fax – photocopy or complete the order form above, and send your credit card details or cheque payable to: Australian Consolidated Press (UK), Moulton Park Business Centre, Red House Road, Moulton Park, Northampton NN3 6AQ, phone (+44) (01) 604 497531, fax (+44) (01) 604 497533, e-mail books@acpmedia.co.uk. Or order online at www.acpuk.com
Non-UK residents: We accept the credit cards listed on the coupon, or cheques, drafts or International Money Orders payable in sterling and drawn on a UK bank. Credit card charges are at the exchange rate current at the time of payment.
Postage and packing UK: Add £1.00 per order plus 25p per book.
Postage and packing overseas: Add £2.00 per order plus 50p per book.
Offer ends 30.06.2006